BEOWULF
and the Beast

Written by Julia Golding

Illustrated by Victor Rivas Villa

Published by Pearson Education Limited, Edinburgh Gate, Harlow, Essex, CM20 2JE
Registered company number: 872828

www.pearsonschools.co.uk

Text © Julia Golding 2012

Designed by Bigtop
Original illustrations © Pearson Education Limited 2012
Illustrated by Victor Rivas Villa

The right of Julia Golding to be identified as author of this work has been asserted by her in
accordance with the Copyright, Designs and Patents Act 1988.

First published 2012

20
10 9

British Library Cataloguing in Publication Data
A catalogue record for this book is available from the British Library

ISBN 978 0 435 07592 7

Printed in China by Golden Cup

Acknowledgements
We would like to thank the children and teachers of Bangor Central Integrated Primary School,
NI; Bishop Henderson C of E Primary School, Somerset; Brookside Community Primary
School, Somerset; Cheddington Combined School, Buckinghamshire; Cofton Primary School,
Birmingham; Dair House Independent School, Buckinghamshire; Deal Parochial School, Kent;
Holy Trinity Catholic Primary School, Chipping Norton; Lawthorn Primary School, North
Ayrshire; Newbold Riverside Primary School, Rugby and Windmill Primary School, Oxford for
their invaluable help in the development and trialling of the Bug Club resources.

Every effort has been made to contact copyright holders of material reproduced in this book.
Any omissions will be rectified in subsequent printings if notice is given to the publisher.

Contents

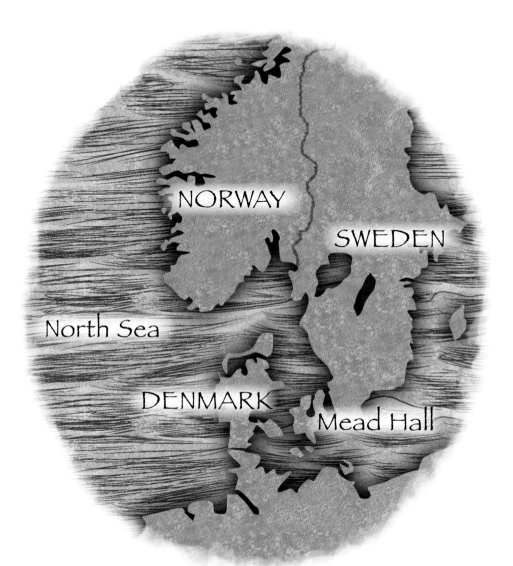

Who was Beowulf?

At some time between the middle of the 8th century and the beginning of the 11th (that means a very, very long time ago), an **Anglo-Saxon** poet wrote down 3000 lines of poetry about a hero called **Beowulf**. It was the superhero tale of its day. Beowulf is the brilliant and brave warrior who goes out in his special uniform of shining armour to fight super-villains; first the monster Grendel, then Grendel's mother and finally, at the end of his life, a dragon (but the dragon is another story!).

The story is set in Denmark not Britain, but maybe the Anglo-Saxons liked hearing about the troubles suffered by their **Viking** neighbours and enemies! We are lucky to have any record of the story at all, as only one copy survived the Middle Ages and that was almost burned in the 18th century.

There are plenty of retellings of the story but there has not been one quite like this. Let's hear from Grendel for once and find out what he has to say for himself …

Chapter One
The Noisy Neighbours

I am Grendel, the grimmest, grungiest, the most garishly ghastly monster of them all, and I have a bone to pick with you humans! You stole my home and I am hopping mad!

Oh, I suppose you have probably heard the tale of the hero, Beowulf, and how he saved the **Danes** and their drinking hall from a monster, blah, blah, blah. The monster in that old story is a demon, burning with anger and a thirst for blood, rampaging through the village in a murderous mood.

All right, I'll put my hand up. I admit I might have caused a little damage by mistake when I got annoyed.

BUT did you ever wonder what caused my anger, or stop to ask if the tale of Beowulf is true? It is not. It is a pack of lies, a story spun by a **bard** to cover up the bad behaviour of the Danes.

This is what really happened …

One day, many years ago, I was enjoying grumbling around my marshy home, scaring the birds off their nests, pottering about the reed beds, and munching on thick, black eels, when I heard the sound of hammering.

Now, you have to understand that this was remarkable because I've always had this rotten part of Denmark mostly to myself. No one else would want to live here, apart from my mum – and that, to be frank, is another reason why humans have avoided our patch. No one – and I mean no one – wants to live with my mother. Not even me.

But I stray from my tale. The hammering. I followed the sound, creeping like a shadow through the undergrowth, poked my head out of the bushes and saw …

… men.

Hundreds of Danes. They had already put up a frame for a huge building. I could see carpenters hanging off the roof, dangling from the walls and digging like badgers to make postholes. They were constructing their new home right on top of my FAVOURITE BREAKFAST SPOT!

Grrrr! Arwaaagh! Had they not heard of the Monstrous
Laws of Planning? This place had been named (by me)
a place of Special Scary Significance. How dare these
people march in and steal my land without even checking
who owned it first!

Blistering beetles! I could do nothing that morning but
curse and fret: there were too many of them and the sun
was up. I am always at my weakest in daylight, my demon
strength sucked out of me like water through a straw. I
would have to wait for my revenge, go into hiding until
these Danes – foolish mortals – went to bed.

Chapter Two
Revenge

I had calmed down by the evening and was ready to consider living in peace with my new neighbours. As long as they kept me happy with the odd sacrifice or two, I would graciously let their invasion pass. A couple of tasty warriors now and again sounded a fair swap to me for my land. Besides, I reasoned, I was ready for a change after hundreds of years of eel pie, eel stew and eel ice cream.

I approached the Danes' hall in a positive mood – that was, until I heard the din.

There are three things I hate more than anything:

1 Loud music   X

2 Drinking songs with stupid words   X

3 Parties to which I have not been invited   X

A celebration was in full swing, everybody enjoying themselves without me. The worst bardic band in **Scandinavia**, the Shieldings, was playing a song that went:

"*Drink **mead** until we fall over*
Drink mead until we fall over
Drink mead until we fall over
And then drink mead some more!"

You can see why I was upset.

But I'm not stupid. I may be a great big, green, bug-eyed fellow with teeth like daggers, but don't let that fool you into thinking I haven't got the brains to plan a battle. I had to wait until every last one of those annoying Danes had staggered to their beds and then …

"Revenge is mine!" I shouted as I burst through the doors into the hall. I grabbed the first three sleepy warriors in one hand and stamped on the fire in the hearth to plunge the room into darkness. Only the angry red light of my eyes was left to pick out my next target. I clutched all five members of the Shieldings in my talons and stormed off, back to my lair.

I will spare you the details, but I will tell you this much: I did the world a favour when I found a use other than music-making for that bardic band.

In my innocence, I thought that would be it. I imagined that the Danes would get the message and move away to build their drinking hall in a place that didn't already belong to someone. But no. That was just the beginning.

They declared war.

Chapter Three
Beowulf's Band Arrives

A few months passed. I successfully kept the noise down at the parties by a few raids, nipping in the bud any sign of a return to the rowdy behaviour of that first feast. I even began to enjoy myself, keeping the Danes on their toes. I did this by random attacks and making loud scary noises at night that kept them lying awake in terror. All good clean fun for a monster.

I did not realise that they were secretly plotting against me. Those stupid Danes! Rather than get the message that they were NOT WANTED in my neck of the woods, they went and called for reinforcements. Grrrr! How thick can they be?

I saw the new men arrive. It was pure luck that I was on the spot when their ship came into sight. I had been doing a bit of fishing for eels down in a lovely little creek that runs into the ocean when I looked up and saw a great big wooden wall approaching.

That couldn't be right.

I rubbed the third of my bug-eyes and looked again. I realised it was a huge ship with a high prow bearing down onto the beach with a scrunch and a crunch. I dived into the bushes and hid.

A Dane ran forward from behind me, holding his sword in front of him. "Whoa, men! Who are you, and why do you come here dressed for battle?" he cried.

I rolled my eyes. How idiotic can you get? If you think they are enemies, one man running up a beach with a puny sword isn't going to scare them off. You need someone like me for that.

"Hail, friend!" shouted the leader of the new arrivals.

Bother – no battle on the beach, then. I sulked.

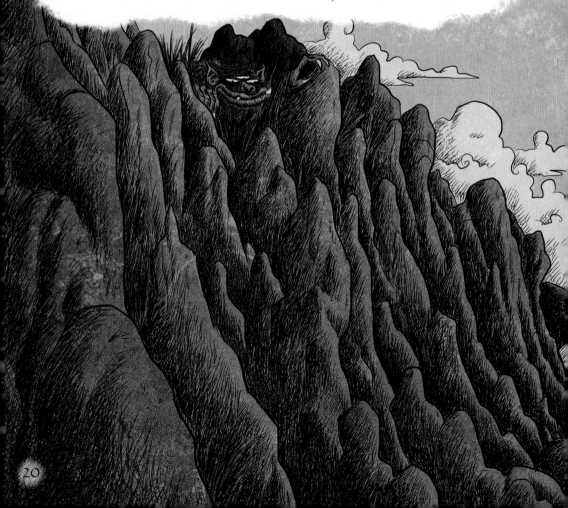

"My name is Beowulf, chief of the **Geats**," continued the leader, "and I come in peace."

I sneaked a look at this Geat. He was big. He was brawny. His armour had been polished so that it shone like a mirror. His helmet was decorated with boars' heads on the cheek-guards. I sniggered: "I guess that makes him pig-headed." I am fond of big warriors as they make a filling meal. Welcome to my land, Beowulf. I look forward to eating you later.

"Wow! Not *the* Beowulf? The winner of Best Warrior in West Denmark three years in a row?" marvelled the Dane.

Beowulf smiled and buffed his nails on his chain-mail shirt.

"Not the Beowulf who slew the sea-beast of South Sweden?" continued the Dane. "Not the Beowulf who was named Most Gorgeous Geat by *Midgard Maiden Magazine*?"

"'Tis I!" Beowulf struck a heroic pose, showing his best side to his admirer. "I heard you had a spot of bother with a monster and I've come to help."

"Oh double-wow! Our king will be so pleased to hear you have come to our rescue. I'll go and tell him right away." The Dane ran off in the direction of the hall.

Beowulf turned his gaze on his followers who had gathered behind him on the beach.

"Now listen, men. We are here on a serious mission. Our task is to fight our toughest monster yet. I do not expect many of us will survive."

A man at the back whimpered.

"Some of us will be eaten."
Two soldiers went green.

"Some will be crushed in wicked claws. The lucky ones among us will have our heads bitten off in one snap of the creature's ferocious jaws. The rest will die slow, gruesome deaths!"

A pale-faced man collapsed in a faint.

"But are we downhearted?"

"No?" came the feeble reply from three of the men still on their feet.

That was not good enough for our hero. "I'll ask you again. Are we downhearted?"

"NO!" the men shouted with more confidence.

"And I'll tell you why: because we are the bravest of the brave, the boldest of the bold. We are Beowulf's Band!"

And then – to my horror – he began to sing a song about beating beasts, swimming with sea-monsters, and defeating devils. His men joined in after the first verse.

I groaned and put my head in my paws. Not another bunch of musical wannabes. The sooner I put an end to their caterwauling, the better for everyone's ears. Beowulf had a date with fate that very night.

Chapter Four
Not Another Party!

In order to keep out of sight,
I needed a cunning disguise.
Thinking quickly, I hid my
monstrous self by speckling
leaves over my sticky skin.
I made an excellent job of
it – no one would recognise
me, not even my mother. I
then followed the band to
the hall. I think Beowulf
suspected they were being
tailed but every time he
turned, I pretended to be
a tree and his eyes slid
right over me.

"Did you hear something, men?" Beowulf asked.

"No, sir," replied his band.

I couldn't blame them: my ears were still ringing from Beowulf's truly terrible singing.

"I could have sworn … but no, that would be foolish. No monster dares come within ten feet of me in broad daylight." Beowulf shook his head and continued walking.

When the Geats reached the hall, the doors were flung open.

"Beowulf!" cried the king of the Danes. "You look just like your father. We were fighting buddies in the good old days."

Beowulf bowed. "I bring his greetings, sire. He told me that he owed you a favour, so I am here in his place. Got a little monster trouble, I understand?"

The king looked glum. "Not little, I'm afraid. So many good strong warriors have come to my hall, promised to stay awake overnight and defend us from the monster but then, next morning …" He grimaced.

"Next morning, what?" asked Beowulf.

"Nothing but a pile of bones and a mess on the floor. All my cleaning staff have resigned. They refused to deal with it any longer."

Beowulf smiled with supreme self-confidence. "Don't worry, sire, I'm here to help. Your problems are at an end."

The king clapped his hands. "In that case, let's have a party!"

I groaned.

Beowulf cupped his ear. "Did you hear that?"

"What?" The king frowned.

"I could have sworn I heard a fiendish growl," said Beowulf.

The king listened. "Nope. I don't hear anything," he said.

Beowulf shook himself. "Oh well. I must still have water in my ears from the voyage. What was that you said about a party?"

The doors to the hall crashed shut behind the Geats and the Danes, locking me out. It did not stop the noise of the party reaching me. Through a little window, I could see them all enjoying themselves, eating, drinking and singing outrageous songs in which the killing of monsters featured very heavily. The king's wife proposed a toast and they all cheered Beowulf – and he hadn't even done anything yet!

It was time that Geat learned he was not so great after all.

Chapter Five
The Battle

All I have ever wanted is a quiet life. I've dreamed of a home where there are plenty of eels to eat and no Mum to nag me. I've even drawn a picture: do you want to see it? Here it is. Notice my little cave with running stream, a cold room for my food and a row of marsh marigolds and wild garlic in the front garden.

Not a human in sight.

Now, thanks to a quirk of fate that had the Danes thinking my land was theirs, I was forced to live alongside a rowdy bunch of neighbours from ... well, you know where! And they called *me* the nightmare! Enough already! I decided I was going to put a stop to their partying that very evening. I was going to go over there to scare the living daylights out of them and send them running for their ships.

Keeping my temper with difficulty, I waited for my opportunity. The revellers sang and danced and ate and drank as if they had already defeated me. I stuck a finger in each ear to try and block out the noise. It was no good.

Finally, the king handed the hall over to Beowulf and his men to guard, and went to bed. The party-goers fell into bed, snoring like thunder. Even the guards were nodding at their posts, having done far too much feasting to remain clear-headed. No one heard me crack open the door – or so I thought. I curled my talons around the edge, scratching the wood with glee.

"Aargh!" I shouted and exploded into the
room. "You will not have parties without me!"

I overturned a table. "You will not sing
stupid songs!"

I threw a keg of mead into the fireplace,
creating a nice whoosh of flame. "And you will
say you are sorry for building on my land!"

I picked up a warrior and yelled in his face.
He screamed and fainted. I threw him aside and
continued with my rampage, thoroughly enjoying
myself. This was pay back, big time.

But then, Beowulf jumped out of the shadows where he had been waiting for me. He didn't have a shield; he didn't have a helmet; he didn't have a sword. What was he playing at?

He jumped onto my back and with bare hands began to throttle me. I was so surprised, I did not react quickly enough. The other warriors used my moment of confusion to strike at me with their swords. Trying to dislodge Beowulf from my back, I bumped from one end of the hall to the other like a rubber ball, but nothing worked. This man stuck to me like glue.

"Let go!" I gasped.

"No, you foul fiend! You have broken up your last feast, party-pooper!" replied Beowulf. "I'm going to tear you limb from limb!"

Now that made me really mad. Flames shot from my nostrils and from my three eyes. I could smell the ends of Beowulf's hair burning, but still he hung on.

"You just don't know when to give up!" I growled, flopping onto my back so that he was squashed to the floor.

The cowardly soldiers did not play by any rules of combat I recognised. They started hitting me.

"Hey, this is single combat!" I shouted. "Not fair."

"No, you are wrong," bellowed Beowulf. "These men are in my band and we act as one, just as we sing as one!"

Now I got really scared. I could tell Beowulf was just itching to break into song. I went limp, all the fight having gone out of me. I must have looked a sight, covered in cuts and bruises. Beowulf wiggled out from under me and stood with his foot on my chest.

"I have conquered Grendel!" he declared.

His men cheered. The king and his men rushed in to see what all the fuss was about.

"This creature can now slither back to his lair and never bother these good Danes again!" added Beowulf.

I took that as my cue to go. I began to crawl for the exit.

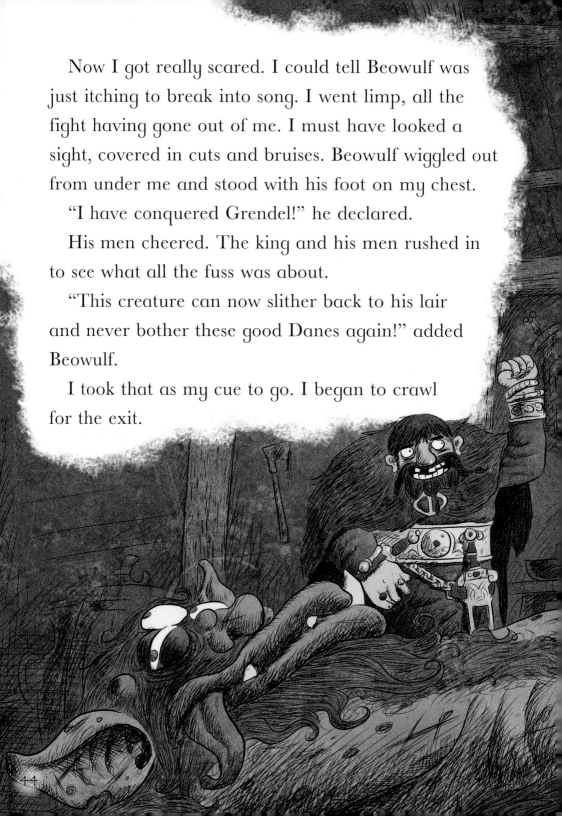

"What!" cried the king. "You are not going to slice and dice him?"

Beowulf turned green. "Oh, yuck! You really would have problems with your cleaners if you get me to butcher a monster in your hall."

The king rubbed his beard. "True. You do have a point." He turned to me. "Be gone, foul beast, and trouble us no more!"

I whimpered, not only because I was hurting everywhere, but also because I could see Beowulf tuning up his harp. Flashing his perfect teeth at the maidens on the front row, he took a breath. I couldn't move fast enough but the torture continued as his song followed me out to my marsh.

"Let's hear three cheers for brave Beowulf,
Three cheers for brave Beowulf,
Three cheers for brave Beowulf,
He saved us all from Grendel!"

I thought that was the end of it, but no, he had a chorus in mind which he got everyone to join in with – everyone, that is, but me!

"Hooray, to the marshes he's banished
Hooray to the marshes he's banished
Hooray to the marshes he's banished
Now it's time to party!"

I did what any self-respecting monster would do in that situation: I turned back at the edge of my swamp and shouted the worst threat I could think of:

"I'm telling my mum!"

With that, I slithered off into the mist to lick my wounds.

Glossary and Pronunciation Guide

Anglo-Saxons   name given to the people who lived in England until the Norman Conquest in 1066

bard   professional poet who composed and recited verses retelling the deeds of brave men; a bard often accompanied himself on the harp or lyre

Beowulf   say 'Bay-o-wolf'

Danes   people who come from Denmark

Geats   say 'Geets'; a sea-faring and warlike tribe who lived in South-West Sweden. Beowulf was their leader

mead   strong drink made from honey and water

Scandinavia   the countries Norway, Sweden and Denmark

Vikings   Scandinavian 'pirates' who raided the coasts of Northern and Western Europe from the 8th to the 11th centuries

Notes on the Songs

In the original poem, Grendel is described as having very sensitive hearing, which explains why he is so upset by the Danes' loud singing and partying.

The song on page 12 is to be sung to the tune of *For He's A Jolly Good Fellow*, and on pages 46-47 to *What Shall We Do With The Drunken Sailor?*

NB: the Vikings were notoriously bad singers! You might find Grendel is not the only one with sensitive ears ...